The Story of a Special Day
Volume 336

December

1

The 335th day of the year (336th in leap years). There are 30 days remaining until the end of the year.

by Michael Dobson

Timespinner
Press

This book is also available in e-book form for Kindle, e-pub devices, and other formats from your favorite online booksellers.

For more information about the series, about us, or about your special day, please email us at editor@timespinnerpress.com.

Look for other volumes in *The Story of a Special Day,* coming often. See www.timespinnerpress.com for details and for the most recent information.

Table of Contents

For the definition of "O.S.," "N.S.," "CE," and "BCE" used with some dates , see the section "On Names and Dates."

Cover: The Montgomery City Bus in which Rosa Parks refused to give up her seat, now located in the Henry Ford Museum, Dearborn, Michigan — for the EVENT OF THE DAY.

Quote of the Day

"People always say that I didn't give up my seat because I was tired, but that isn't true. I was not tired physically, or no more tired than I usually was at the end of a working day. I was not old, although some people have an image of me as being old then. I was forty-two. No, the only tired I was, was tired of giving in."

Rosa Parks, civil rights activist who refused to give up her bus seat to a white man, triggering the Montgomery Bus Boycott, December 1, 1955

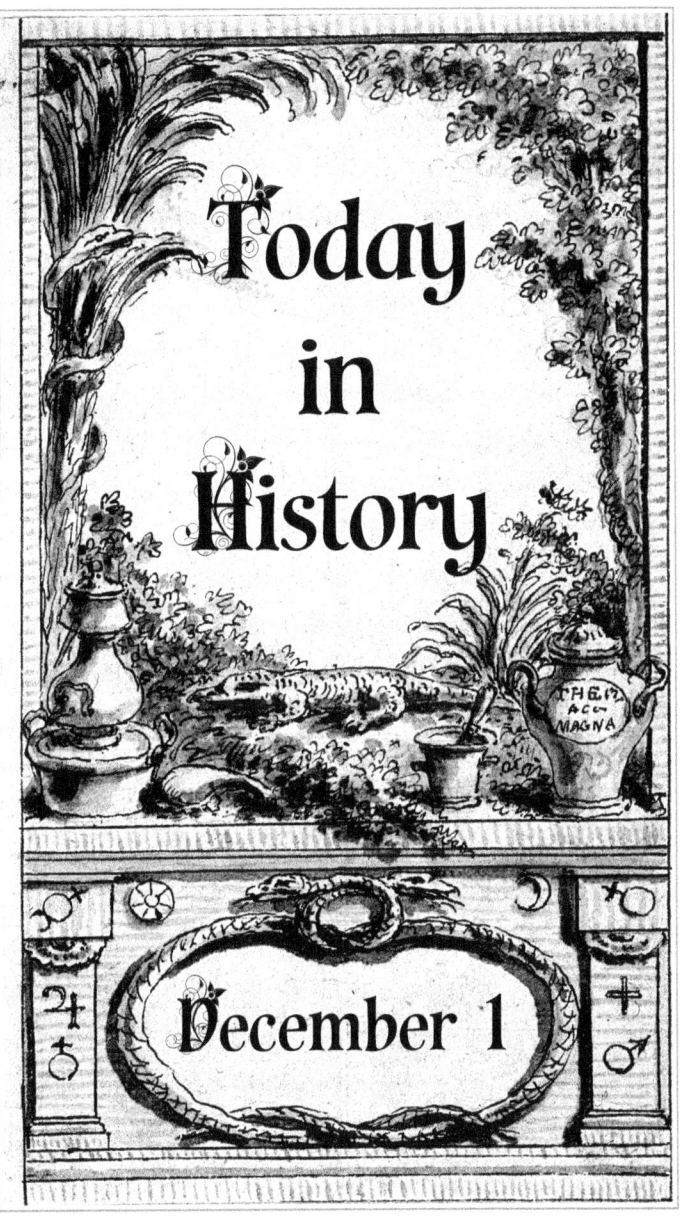

Today
in
History

December 1

Rosa Parks in 1955, with Dr. Martin Luther King, Jr., in the
background. (National Archives)

Rosa Parks Refuses to Give Up Her Seat on the Bus

On December 1, 1955, Montgomery, Alabama, seamstress Rosa Parks refused to give up her bus seat to a white man, and was arrested. This triggered the Montgomery Bus Boycott, a key moment in the civil rights struggle in the American South.

Segregation in the American South

Although the abolition of slavery and the passage of the 13th, 14th, and 15th amendments to the US Constitution officially made citizens of African-Americans, actions by the former Confederate states had turned back much of that progress through what became known as "Jim Crow" laws. Jim Crow laws (officially labeled "separate but equal," though they were anything but equal) enforced racial segregation in all public facilities, from schools to drinking fountains. The right to vote was routinely denied through such mechanisms as the poll tax and literacy requirements, frequently backed up by lynchings.

Montgomery Bus Rules

In 1900, Montgomery, Alabama, established a city ordinance requiring segregation on public buses. The first four rows of each bus were reserved for whites, and the "colored" section began at the back. Black passengers entered the front door of the bus to pay their fares, then had to exit and reenter via the back door. The boundary between the white and "colored" section was indicated with a movable sign. If the whites-only seats filled up, the sign was moved backward. Any blacks sitting on those seats were required to surrender them to white passengers. Because blacks made up three-fourths of the ridership, this frequently meant that black passengers would have to stand when there were empty seats in the white section.

The Refusal

At the end of a long day at work, seamstress Rosa Parks boarded the Cleveland Avenue bus around six o'clock in the evening on Thursday, December 1, 1955. She paid her fare and sat in the first row in the colored section. As the bus continued along its route, the white-only seats filled up and soon there were a few white people standing. The bus driver moved the dividing sign to add seats to the whites-only section, ordering Parks and three other passengers to give up their seats.

"I felt a determination to cover my body like a quilt on a winter night," Rosa Parks said later. "I thought of [murdered teenager] Emmett Till and I just couldn't go back."

Faced with her refusal to move, the bus driver said, "Well, if you don't stand up, I'm going to have to call the police and have you arrested."

"You may do that," she replied. He did so, and

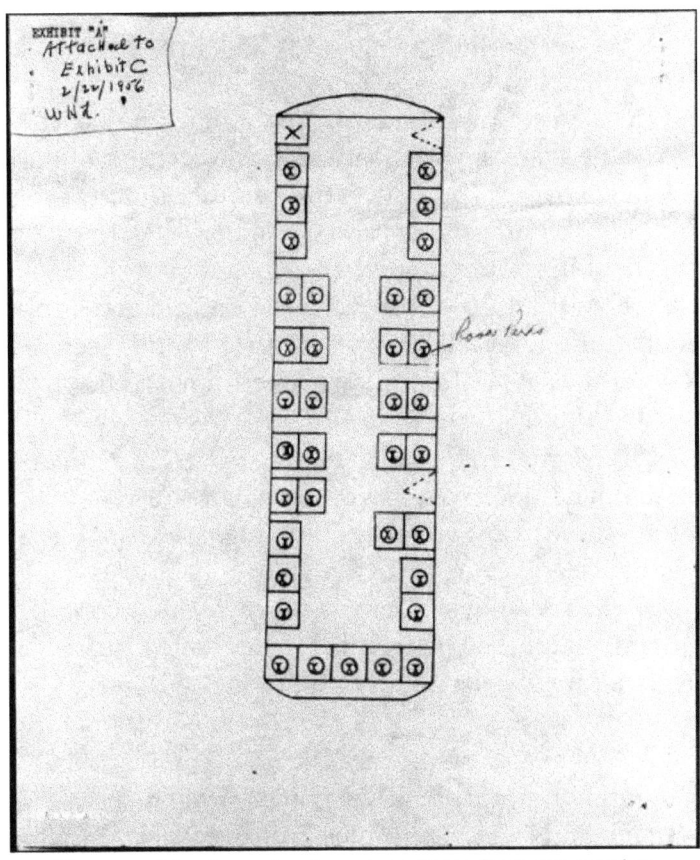

Diagram of the bus, showing where Rosa Park sat, used as
evidence in the Browder v. Gayle case (National Archives)

she was indeed arrested and charged with a violation of the segregation law. The president of the Montgomery chapter of the NAACP bailed her out of jail the next evening.

The Montgomery Bus Boycott

Rosa Park was already involved in the nascent civil rights movement. She was local secretary of the NAACP chapter and had participated in fund raising and other campaigns for equal justice. A meeting was held in a Montgomery church, led by local pastor Martin Luther King., Jr. The group agreed to a boycott of the Montgomery bus system, and elected Rev. King as its leader. They printed some 35,000 handbills and spread the word.

The Montgomery Bus Boycott officially began on December 5, 1955, the day of Rosa Parks' trial, in which she was convicted of violating a segregation ordinance and fined $10, plus $4 in court costs. It would last 381 days, finally coming to an end on December 20, 1956, when the US Supreme Court declared that Alabama and Montgomery laws requiring segregated buses were unconstitutional.

Rather than ride the bus, African-Americans in Montgomery hitchhiked, carpooled, rode bicycles, walked, and even rode mules or drove horse-drawn buggies. Black taxi drivers charged ten cents a ride to boycotters, the same price as a bus ride. The local bus systems experienced a dramatic drop in revenue and found itself in financial distress.

The city fought back. Local insurance companies were pressured to stop insuring carpool cars. City officials attempted to fine any taxi driver charging less than 45¢. White segregationists formed the White Citizens' Council, a supposedly respectable alternative to the Ku Klux Klan, and members firebombed the homes of Dr. King and Ralph Abernathy, along with four black Baptist churches. Boycotters were physically attacked, and boycott leaders, including Dr. King, were indicted for "conspiring to interfere with a business." Ordered to pay a $500 fine, King elected to go to jail, an act that brought national attention to the protest.

Browder v. Gayle

Because the Rosa Parks case had to go through the Alabama court system before it could be appealed at the Federal level, the NAACP Legal Defense Fund decided to used a different case. Aurelia Browder had been arrested for the same offense about eight months before Rosa Parks, and became the plaintiff in *Browder v. Gayle*, a lawsuit filed in the US District Court. This resulted in a ruling that segregated buses violated the Equal Protection clause of the 14th Amendment and were therefore unconstitutional, a decision subsequently affirmed by the US Supreme Court.

Victory was accompanied by more violence. A shotgun was fired through the front door of Dr. King's home. On Christmas Eve of that year, white men attacked a black teenager as she exited a bus. Snipers fired on two buses, and a pregnant woman was shot in both legs. Five more black churches were bombed. While the Montgomery Bus Boycott was a victory, it changed very little about the reality of day-to-day segregation in Alabama at the time. However, as a key moment in the civil rights struggle, its effects over time were important.

The Aftermath

Rosa Parks was fired from her department store job, and her husband was forced out of his for speaking up. She received death threats and other sanctions. In 1957, she and her husband left Montgomery, first for Hampton, Virginia, and later to Detroit, Michigan, where she would live until her death in 2005. She worked as a secretary to Congressman John Conyers for many years, and remained a civil rights activist throughout her life.

She received numerous honors throughout her lifetime, including the Presidential Medal of Freedom, the Congressional God Medal, and the NAACP Spingarn Medal. The bus on which she was riding is now on display at the Henry Ford Museum in Dearborn, Michigan.

Roads, schools, and parks have been named for her. In 1994, the Ku Klux Klan applied to sponsor cleanup activities on part of Interstate 55 in Missouri, which would allow them to post signs showing the involvement of their organization. Unable to refuse KKK sponsorship under the law, the Missouri State Legislature instead voted to rename the section as "Rosa Parks Highway." The Klan lost its sponsorship rights in 2001, on the grounds that not once did they actually clean the freeway.

President Barack Obama sitting in
the Rosa Parks bus (Photo: Pete Souza

Christine Jorgensen (Photo: Maurice Seymour)

What Happened on December 1?

From the creation of great works of engineering and art, to devastating wars and natural disasters, thousands of years of history have left their mark on each and every day of the year. Here are some important events that occurred on December 1. (Items with a photo or illustration are boxed.)

1824 — For the first and only time in US history, **no candidate for president won a majority of votes in the Electoral College, sending the decision to the House of Representatives,** which chose John Quincy Adams over Andrew Jackson to be the 6th President of the United States.

1865 — **Shaw University**, the first historically black university in the southern US, **is founded** in Raleigh, North Carolina.

1941 — The **Civil Air Patrol** is created.

1952 — The New York *Daily News* announces that **Christine Jorgensen had undergone sex-reassignment surgery,** making her the first major spokesperson for transgendered people.

1959 — The **Antarctic Treaty System**, establishing the continent as a scientific preserve and banning military activity, is opened for signature.

1960 — Beatles **Paul McCartney and Pete Best are arrested** in Hamburg (and subsequently deported) **on charges of arson** after setting a condom on fire in a club hallway.

1990 — In the construction of the Channel Tunnel, **the tunnel sections drilled from the English and the French sides finally connect.**

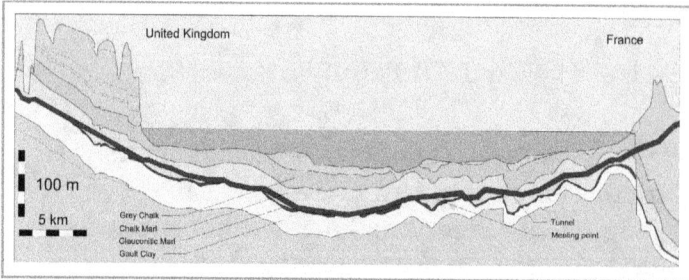

Geographical profile of the Channel Tunnel, showing the meeting point where the French and English sides first connected. (Artist: Commander Keane, CC BY-SA 4.0)

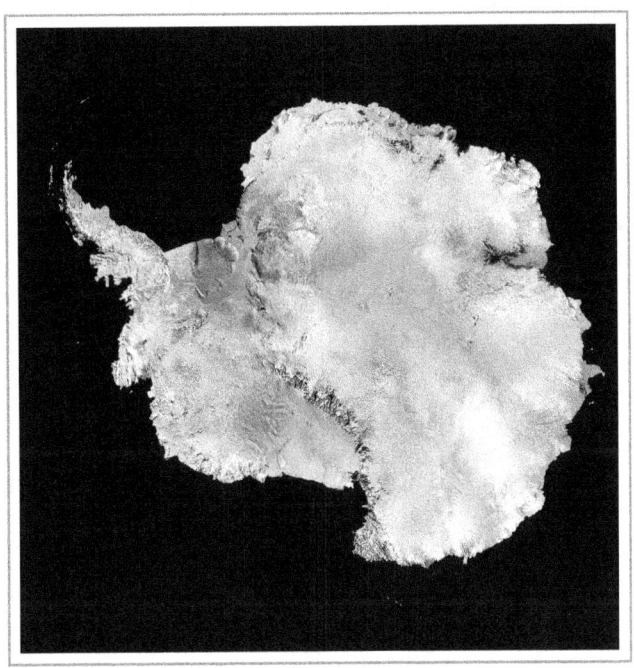

Antarctica (Photo: Dave Papp)

Quote of the Day

"If an expert says it can't be done, get another expert."

David Ben-Gurion, first Prime Minister of Israel
died December 1, 1973

Births and Deaths

December 1

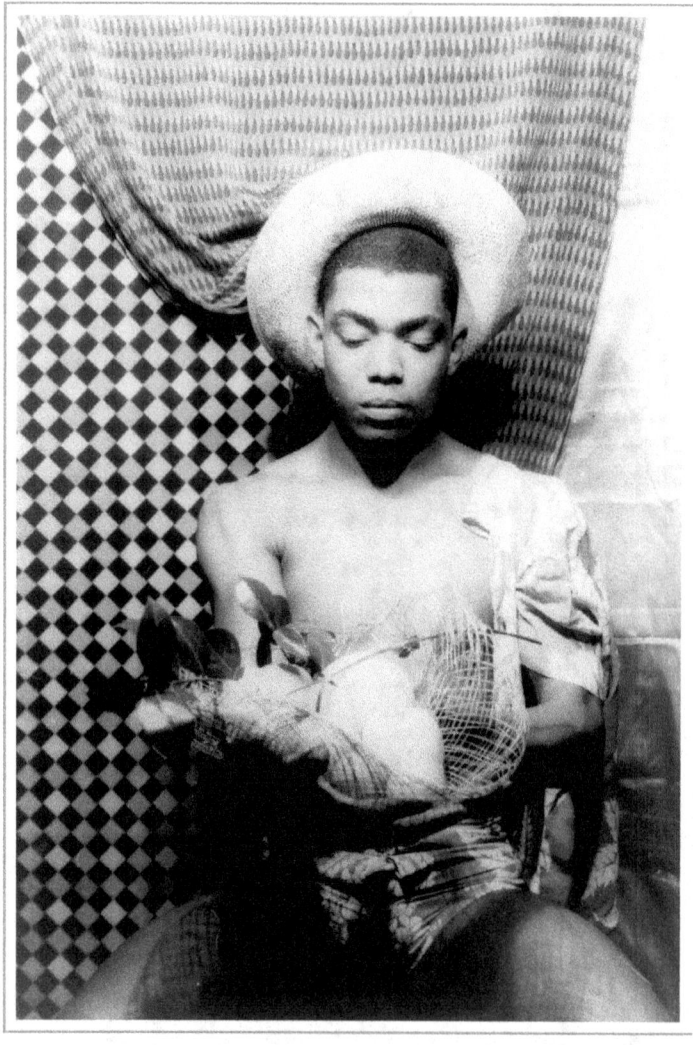

Alvin Ailey, choreographer and dancer,
winner of the Presidential Medal of Freedom, died December 1,
1989. (Photo: Carl Van Vechten)

Notable December 1 People

With the current world population at about seven billion people, on average about 19 million people also celebrate their birthdays on December 1 — and that isn't counting millions and millions who came before! No matter when you were born, you share your birthday with many special people whose accomplishments (and occasionally embarrassments) have been noted as part of history.

In this section, you'll meet fascinating people who share your birthday. They're organized by what they're famous for, and then in reverse chronological order from most recent to earliest. Those who are shown in photographs or artwork have a box around them. We don't have photos of everyone, so please forgive us if your favorite person is missing.

Some of these people you've heard of, others will be new to you, but they all make up an important part of the reason that December 1 is a truly special day!

Michelini Bernardini modeling the first bikini (1946)

Who Was Born on December 1?

Business and Technology

Safra A. Catz, female business executive made co-CEO of Oracle Corporation in 2014. *(1961)*

Minoru Yamasaki, architect who designed the the original New York World Trade Center. *(1912)*

Marie Tussaud, artist known for her wax sculptures, founded Madame Tussaud's Wax Museum. *(1761)*

Fashion and Modeling

Carol Alt, supermodel who appeared on nearly 500 magazine covers, including the 1982 *Sports Illustrated* swimsuit issue. *(1960)*

Micheline Bernardini, nude dancer famous as the model for the 1946 unveiling of the first bikini (named for an atomic test in the Bikini Atoll), because no "respectable" model would wear it. *(1921)*

Military

Vernon McGarity, American sergeant who won the Medal of Honor for his actions on the first day of the Battle of the Bulge. *(1921)*

Гео́ргий Константи́нович Жу́ков (Georgy Zhukov), Soviet military leader who served as Chief of the General Staff, Minister of Defense, and Politburo member during and after World War II. *(1896 [O.S.[1] 19 November])*

Music and Dance

Brad Delson, lead guitarist for the band Linkin Park. *(1977)*

Gilbert O'Sullivan, singer-songwriter best known for his 1972 hit "Alone Again (Naturally)." *(1946)*

Bette Midler, "the Divine Miss M," singer-songwriter, actress, and comedienne known for such hits as "Do You Want to Dance," "Boogie Woogie Bugle Boy," and "The Rose," title song of the film of the same name. *(1945)*

John Densmore, drummer for The Doors. *(1944)*

Lou Rawls, singer best known for such hits as "You'll Never Find Another Love Like Mine" and "Wind Beneath My Wings." *(1933)*

---

[1] [1] For the meaning of "O.S.," see "On Names and Dates."

Marshal Georgy Zhukov on the cover of Life magazine, July 31, 1944. (Photo: Gregory Weil)

Matt Monro, English pop vocalist known for such hits as the title song from the 1963 James Bond film *From Russia With Love* and 1966's *Born Free. (1930)*

Alicia Markova, *prima ballerina assoluta,* considered to be one of the greatest 20th century classical ballet dancers. *(1910)*

Performing Arts

Sarah Silverman, comedienne and television producer best known for her Emmy-nominated *The Sarah Silverman Program* and for roles in such films as *School of Rock* and *I Smile Back. (1970)*

Nestor Carbonell, actor best known as Richard Albert from the television series *Lost* and as Mayor Garcia in the Batman films *The Dark Knight* and *The Dark Knight Rises. (1967)*

Andrew Adamson, filmmaker known for his Academy nominated *Shrek* and *Shrek 2* films.

Treat Williams, actor who first came to stardom in the 1979 film *Hair,* also known for such films as *Prince of the City* and *Once Upon a Time in America. (1951)*

Richard Keith, child actor known for playing "Little Ricky" in the sitcom *I Love Lucy.* (1950)

Jonathan Katz, best known as the star of the animated sitcom *Dr. Katz, Professional Therapist. (1946)*

Richard Pryor, African-American comedian, social critic, and actor; awarded the first Kennedy Center Mark Twain Prize for American Humor in 1998. *(1940)* *(Photo next page)*

Woody Allen, comedian, actor, writer, and filmmaker, winner of four Academy Awards and numerous other honors. *(1935)* *(Photo next page)*

David Doyle, actor best known for his role as Bosley on the 1970s television series *Charlie's Angels. (1929)*

Malachi Throne, actor best known for his role as Noah Bain on the 1960s television series *It Takes a Thief. (1928)*

Emily McLaughlin, actress known for her long-time role as Nurse Jessie on the soap opera *General Hospital. (1928)*

Mary Martin, actress who originated such roles as Nellie Forbush in *South Pacific*, Maria von Trapp in *The Sound of Music*, and the title role in *Peter Pan*. Member of the American Theater Hall of Fame, Kennedy Center Honors, mother of actor Larry Hagman. *(1913)*

Cyril Richard, stage, screen, and television actor best known for playing Captain Hook in the 1954 musical production of *Peter Pan*, starring Mary Martin, also born on December 1. *(1898)*

Richard Pryor (right) with Alan Alda and Lily Tomlin, from the 1973 CBS special *Lily*.

Woody Allen (center) with Diane Keaton and Jerry Lacy from the Broadway run of *Play It Again, Sam*.

Science and Medicine

Martin Rodbell, biochemist who shared the 1994 Nobel Prize in Physiology or Medicine for discovering the role certain proteins played in sending signals among cells. *(1925)*

William F. House, medical researcher who developed the cochlear implant, restoring the sense of hearing in many cases. *(1923)*

Николай Иванович Лобачевский (Nikolai Lobachevsky), mathematician known for developing hyperbolic geometry, and for a 1953 satirical Tom Lehrer song, "Lobachevsky." Although the song accuses the mathematician of plagiarism, Lehrer stated that the name was chosen merely for its sound, and is "not intended as a slur on [Lobachevsky's] character." *(1792 [O.S.[2] 20 November])*

Martin Klaproth, chemist who discovered the elements uranium, zirconium, and cerium. *(1743)*

Sports

孫楊 **(Sun Yang),** first Chinese man to win an Olympic gold medal in swimming, and first in history to receive Olympic gold in the 200, 400, and 1500 meter freestyle events. *(1991)*

---

[2] For the meaning of "O.S.," see "On Names and Dates."

Stephanie Brown Trafton, won an Olympic gold medal in discus throwing. *(1979)*

Nathalie Lambert, Olympic gold medalist in speed skating, three-time world champion. *(1963)*

Wally Lewis, rugby player known as the "Emperor of Long Park," named a Legend of Australian Sport. *(1959)*

Pat Spillane, Irish footballer (soccer player) considered one of the greatest of all time. *(1955)*

Lee Trevino, legendary golfer and member of the World Golf Hall of Fame. *(1939)*

Calvin Griffith, owner of the Washington Senators/ Minneapolis Twins baseball franchise for nearly 30 years. *(1911)*

Walter "Smokey" Alston, baseball player and manager best known for managing the Brooklyn/ Los Angeles Dodgers from 1954 to 1976, elected to the Baseball Hall of Fame in 1983. *(1911)*

Writing

Jo Walton, fantasy and science fiction writer whose 2010 novel *Among Others* won both the Hugo Award and the Nebula Award. *(1964)*

Candace Bushnell, whose New York *Observer* column was collected into the best-selling *Sex and the City,* made into a hit television series. *(1958)*

Lee Trevino (Photo: Keith Allison)

Douglas Niles, fantasy author and H. G. Wells Award-winning game designer, known for his fantasy novels and his military thrillers, including *Fox on the Rhine* and *MacArthur's War* (with Michael Dobson). *(1964)*

John Crowley, winner of the World Fantasy Award for his 1981 classic *Little, Big. (1942)*

Rex Stout, mystery writer who created the detective Nero Wolfe, named a Grand Master of the Mystery Writers of America. *(1886)*

Julia A. Moore, American poet famed for her bad poetry, so bad that one critic wrote, "Shakespeare, could he read it, would be glad that he was dead ... If Julia A. Moore would kindly deign to shed some of her poetry on our humble grave, we should be but too glad to go out and shoot ourselves tomorrow." *(1847)*

Illustration of Rex Stout's Nero Wolfe from the December 1938 issue of *The American Magazine.* (Artist: Ronald McLeod)

David Ben-Gurion (Photo: Pinn Hans, courtesy Israel National
Photo Collection)

Who Died on December 1?

Government and Military

Edward Heffron, US Army private during World War II, character in the book and television series *Band of Brothers*. (2013)

Freeman V. Horner, US Army sergeant who won the Medal of Honor for single-handedly taking out three German machine gun positions during World War II. *(2005)*

Gust Avarkotos, CIA case officer who wrote the 2003 book *Charlie Wilson's War,* made into a 2007 film of the same name, in which he was played by Philip Seymour Hoffman. *(2005)*

David Ben-Gurion, primary founder of the state of Israel and its first prime minister. (1973)

Alfred Thayer Mahan, US Navy admiral, historian, and strategist; author of the 1890 book *The Influence of Sea Power Upon History, 1660-1783,* which continues to influence naval strategists worldwide. *(1914)*

George Everett, Surveyor-General of India, namesake of Mount Everest. *(1866)*

Music and Dance

Stéphane Grappelli, French jazz violinist who co-founded the Quintette du Hot Club de France with guitarist Django Reinhardt; recorded with artists as diverse as Yehudi Menuhin, Paul Simon, Dave Grisman, and Jean-Luc Ponty. *(1997)*

Alvin Ailey, African-American choreographer and activist, founder of the Alvin Ailey American Dance Theater and winner of the Presidential Medal of Freedom. *(1989) (Photo page 14)*

Performing Arts

Paul Benedict, actor particularly known for playing neighbor Harry Bentley on the 1970s sitcom *The Jeffersons. (2008)*

Susanna Centlivre, Englishwoman known as the most successful female playwright of the 18th century. *(1848)*

Science and Mathematics

George Stigler, won the Nobel Memorial Prize in Economics. *(1991)*

J. B. S. Haldane, scientist known for his work in the fields of genetics, evolutionary biology, and biostatistics, known for his "primordial soup" theory of the chemical origin of life. *(1964)*

Stéphane Grappelli (Photo: Allan Warren, CC BY-SA 3.0)

Sports

Jovan Belcher, football linebacker particularly remembered for the murder of his girlfriend and his own subsequent suicide. *(2012)*

Ken McGregor, tennis player, partner of Frank Sedgman, ranked as high as World No. 3, member of the International Tennis Hall of Fame. (2007)

Eugenio Monti, Italian bobsledder who won ten World Championship medals (nine gold) and six Olympic medals (two gold). *(2003)*

Punch Imlach, NHL coach and general manager, member of the Hockey Hall of Fame. *(1987)*

Nellie Fox, second baseman for the Philadelphia Athletics, the Chicago White Sox, and the Houston Astros; member of the Baseball Hall of Fame. *(1975)*

Writing

Edward L. Beach, Jr., US Navy submarine officer during World War II, winner of the Navy Cross, authored the novel *Run Silent, Run Deep*, made into a film in 1958. *(2002)*

James Baldwin, African-American novelist, poet, and social critic known for such works as *Go Tell it on the Mountain, Notes of a Native Son,* and *The Fire Next Time. (1987)*

Anna Roosevelt Halsted, journalist and newspaper editor, daughter of US President Franklin D. Roosevelt and First Lady Eleanor Roosevelt. *(1975)*

Aleister Crowley, influential English occultist and writer described as "the wickedest man in the world." *(1947)*

José Eustasio Rivera, wrote the Venezuelan national epic *The Vortex*, considered one of the most important works of Latin American literature. *(1928)*

Aleister Crowley as a young man (image created by"Magikritualnacht," CC BY-SA 3.0)

Quote of the Day

"I was thrown out of college for cheating on the metaphysics exam; I looked into the soul of the boy sitting next to me."

Woody Allen, filmmaker and comedian, born December 1, 1935

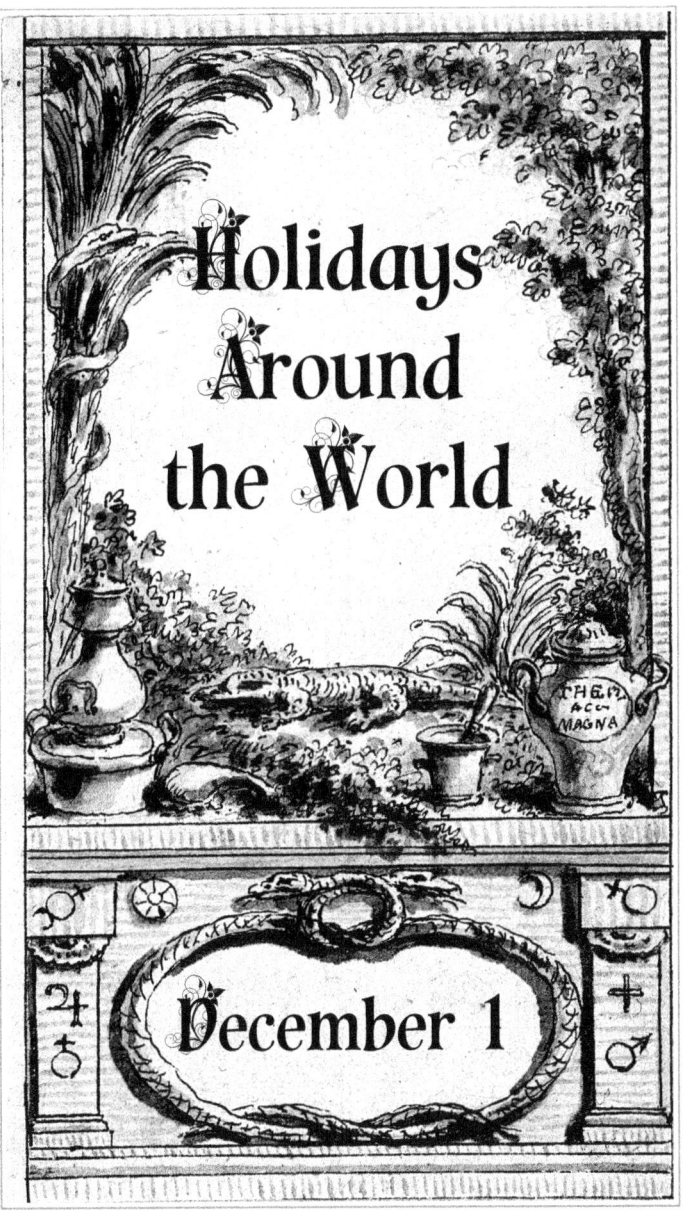

Holidays Around the World

December 1

Coronation of Portuguese King John IV, by Veloso Salgado — for
RESTAURAÇÃO DA INDEPENDÊNCIA DAY

Holidays Around the World

If you're looking for a reason to take your special day off, you should know that every single day is a holiday somewhere in the world! Here's some of what you can celebrate on December 1!

General Events

Freedom and Democracy Day (Chad)

Government offices and businesses in Chad close on December 1 to commemorate he overthrow of Hissène Habré by Idriss Déby in 1990.

Fullveldisdagurinn (Iceland)

Self-Governance Day is observed each year on December 1 in Iceland.

Military Abolition Day (Costa Rica)

On December 1, 1948, President President José Figueres Ferrer of Costa Rica abolished the military of Costa Rica after victory in the civil war in that year.

Restauração da Independência (Portugal)

Restoration of Independence Day commemorates the 1640-1668 war between Portugal and Spain that led to the reestablishment of the Kingdom of Portugal as a kingdom independent from Spain.

Republic Day (Central African Republic)

Celebrates the establishment of the Central African Republic as an autonomous republic in the French community, which took place December 1, 1958.

Rosa Parks Day (California, Missouri, Ohio, Oregon)

Rosa Parks Day (see the "Event of the Day") is an official observance in four US states. In California and Missouri, it takes place on February 4, the birthday of Rosa Parks, and in Ohio and Oregon it takes place on December 1, the date of her arrest.

Teacher's Day (Panama)

Many nations set aside a day each year to honor the contribution of teachers. In Panama, December 1 commemorates the birthday of Manuel José Hurtado, known as the father of Panamanian education for establishing the first public schools and teachers' colleges in that nation.

Тұңғыш Президент күні (Tungysh President kuny) (Kazakhstan)

in Kazakhstan, December 1 is observed as First President Day. As there has only been (at the time of writing) one President of Kazakhstan, Nursultan Nazarbayev, First President Day honors him.

Wan Damrong Rachanuphap (Thailand)

Prince Damrong Rachanuphap Day commemorates the death of Prince Damrong Rajanubbhab (spellings vary), who founded the Thai educational system.

World AIDS Day (UN World Health Organization)

The World Health Organization of the United Nations performs eight official global public health campaigns each year, with awareness of the AIDS pandemic taking place on December 1 each year.

Ziua Marii Uniri (Romania)

The union of Transylvania with Romania in 1818 is celebrated as Great Union Day.

Prince Damrong Rajanubhab —
for DAMRONG RACHANUPHAP DAY

Food Holidays

In the United States, almost every day of the year is dedicated to a particular food. (Some other countries also have official food days, but only in America is there one every single day!) Sponsored by manufacturers, retailers, farmers, or simply fans, these days are often proclaimed by the President, Congress, state governors, or mayors. Given that there are more different foods than days of the year, some days honor more than one kind of food!

In the US, December 1 is **National Eat a Red Apple Day** according to some sources, and **National Fried Pie Day** according to others. If you eat some fried apple pie, you can celebrate both at the same time! The website Foodimentary also lists December 1 as **National French Fried Clams Day,** though we'd prefer not to eat them with our fried apple pies.

If December 1 is the first Saturday of the month, it's also **National Rhubarb Vodka Day**. Drink enough, and it won't matter whether fried clams decorate your fried apple pie or not.

In addition, the entire month of December is used to celebrate numerous foods.With Christmas on the horizon, it shouldn't be surprising that December is ! **National Egg Nog Month** and **National Fruit Cake Month**. You could, we suppose, make your egg nog and fruit cake using rhubarb vodka, but we prefer more traditional tipples.

And while we're on the subject of food, it's also **Food Service Safety Month**. The first week in December is also **National Handwashing Week**, which is clearly related to food safety.

"Landscape with Apple Tree," by Levi Wells Prentice
for NATIONAL EAT A RED APPLE DAY

Religious Feast Days and Holidays

Saint Days

Each day in the year is considered a feast day for one or more saints. They are somewhat different in western Christianity (Catholicism and many forms of Protestantism) and in eastern (Orthodox) Christianity. There are many others; this is a selection.

In *Western Christianity*, December 1 is the feast day of Blessed Bruna Pellesi and Charles de Foucauld, along with saints Castritian, Eligius, Edmund Campion, and Nicholas Ferrar (Episcopal Church).

In *Eastern Orthodox Christianity*, it is also the commemoration of the Prophet Nahum; Saints Onesimus, Ananias, Solochonus, Porphyrios, Anthony the New, Grwst the Confessor, and Theokletos. (These people are honored on November 18 by "Old Calendrists.")

Honorary Months

Presidents, Congresses, and nations around the world issue proclamations recognizing particular months to honor certain causes. These events generally fall in December, though honorary months do come and go. Holidays established by states and nonprofit organizations are listed if verified. If not otherwise specified, all months are US. There is some variation from year to year; some celebratory months get added and others get dropped. Two places to get up to date information are the current edition of *Chase's Calendar of Events* or the website Brownielocks. Here are some honorary designations for December.

- Bingo's Birthday Month (the game, not the dog)

- National Critical Infrastructure Protection Month
- National Impaired Driving Prevention Month
- National Sign Up for Summer Camp Month
- National Stress-Free Family Holiday Month
- Safe Toys and Gifts Month
- Spiritual Literacy Month
- Universal Human Rights Month
- Write a Business Plan Month

Bingo card (Photo: Abbey Hendrickson, CC BY-SA 2.0) — for BINGO'S BIRTHDAY MONTH

B	I	N	G	O
12	25	41	51	63
3	30	37	54	66
7	21	FREE	56	74
1	26	35	50	69
10	17	45	47	64

Moveable and Multi-Day Events

Some events take place over a specific week or time period. Start and finish dates may vary from year to year. Some events occur on different days each year (such as "fourth Saturday of a month"). These events sometimes take place on December 1.

First Week in December (starts any day from December 1-7)

- Cookie Cutter Week (for collectors of cookie cutters)
- National Hand Washing Awareness Week

First Friday in December (December 1-7)

- Farmer's Day (Ghana)
- Faux Fur Friday
- Gospel Day (Marshall Islands)
- National Salesperson Day

First Saturday in December (December 1-7)

- Bartender Appreciation Day
- Earmuff Day

First Sunday in December (December 1-7)

- Good Neighborliness Day (Turkmenistan)

Advent (Christianity)

The four weeks prior to Christmas are known as the Advent season, a time of expectant waiting and preparation for the celebration of the Nativity of Jesus.

A large advent calendar in Germany
(Photo: Kora27, CC BY-SA 4.0)

Hanukkah (חֲנֻכָּה) (Judaism)

The Jewish celebration of Hanukkah, also known as the Festival of Lights or the Feast of Dedication, takes place for eight days and nights beginning on the 25th day of Kislev, which varies from late November to late December. It commemorates the rededication of the Second Temple in Jerusalem at the time of the Maccabean Revolt.

Each night of Hanukkah is marked by lighting one branch of the Menorah, a candelabrum with nine branches. In addition to prayers, celebrants eat foods fried or baked in olive oil. Children play with a spinning top known as a dreidel and receive Hanukkah gelt.

18th century painting of a Hanukkah celebration, artist unknown.

Karthikai Deepam (கார்த்திகை விளக்கீடு) (Hindu Tamil)

The Hindu Tamil celebration of Karthikai Deepam takes place in mid-November to mid-December when the moon is in conjunction with the Pleiades *(Karthigai)*. It is a religious festival of lamps and also celebrates the bonding between brothers and sisters.

Just for Fun

Anybody can make up a holiday, and many people do! While none of these are officially recognized and some may come and go, here are a few more holidays for December 1.

- Antarctica Day
- Baskeball Day
- Civil Air Patrol Day

Quote of the Day

"Ooh, with a little luck —
December will be magic again."

Kate Bush, singer-songwriter
"December Will be Magic Again"

About
the
Month
of

December

"December," from the *Brevarium Grimani* by Simon Bening (c.1510)

December: The Twelfth Month

"In cold December fragrant chaplets blow,
And heavy harvests nod beneath the snow."

— Alexander Pope, *Dunciad*.

In Latin, *decem* means "ten," so it may seem strange that December is actually the twelfth month of the year. The original Roman calendar, from which our month names come, began in March, making December indeed the tenth month.

No one is completely sure when the start of the year was moved to January, but the traditional name of December stuck.

In the northern hemisphere, December is the month with the shortest daylight hours of the year; in the southern hemisphere, it's the opposite. December is the equivalent of June in the southern hemisphere, and vice versa.

In the Julian and Gregorian calendars, December is the twelfth and last month of the year, and is one of seven months with 31 days.

In every year, December starts on the same day of the week as September, and ends on the same day of the week as April.

The length of the day varies through the year, because the Earth tilts as it revolves around the Sun. The two extremes are known as the *solstices*, and the points at which day and night are of equal length are known as the *equinoxes*. The northern hemisphere's winter solstice, which is the shortest day of the year, falls in December. In the southern hemisphere, the summer solstice, the longest day of the year, falls in December.

The dates of the solstice can vary between December 20 and 22. Because even the ancients could tell when the days stopped getting shorter (or longer) and started in the other direction, many holidays and festivals take place around the time of the solstice, including most famously Christmas.

"December," by Gabriel Perelle

December in Other Cultures

In Albanian, the month of December is known as *Dhjetor.* In Egyptian Arabic, it's ديسمبر (pronounced *dīsambar*). In Czech, it's *Prosinec,* in Finland it's *Joulukuu,* and in Poland it's *Grudzień.* Hungarians say *Karácsony hava.*

In Greek, the month of Δεκέμβριος is pronounced *Dekémbrios.* In Hebrew, it's דצמבר and Hindi, it's दिसंबर.

In Irish Gaelic, the month of December is *Nollaig mi na Nollag* and in Scottish Gaelic it's *an Dùbhlachd.* The Welsh say *Rhagfyr.*

The Chinese and Japanese both write the month 十二月, but it is pronounced differently in Cantonese, Mandarin, and Japanese. Koreans write it as 십이월, or *Sipiweol.* In Vietnam it's 腩迚乞 *(Tháng mười hai).*

In Old English, the month is *Gēolmōnaþ* and in Anglo-Saxon it's *Ærra-ġēola mōnaþ.*

The month of December does not correspond exactly with months in other calendar systems. The Hebrew months of כִּסְלֵו *(Kislev)* and טֵבֵת *(Tevet)* overlap December, as do the Persian months of آذر *(Azar)* and دی *(Dey)* and the Hindu months of मार्गशीर्ष *(Mārgaśirṣa)* and पूस *(Pauṣa).*

In the Islamic world, the lunar calendar consists of 354 or 355 days, meaning that the months slowly migrate through the year, and over time different months correspond to December.

December Sayings and Superstitions

- "A green December fills the graveyard."
- "When December snows fall fast, marry and true love will last."
- "A December bride will be fond of novelty, entertaining but extravagant."
- "Married in days of December's cheer / Love's star shines brighter from year to year."

Which day should you marry? That's easy.

> "Monday for health
> Tuesday for wealth
> Wednesday best of all
> Thursday for losses
> Friday for crosses
> Saturday for no luck at all."

According to legend, auspicious dates for December weddings are 1, 8, 10, 19, 23, and 29.

December Symbols

Birthstone: December birthstones in various traditions include turquoise, lapiz lazuli, zircon, blue topaz, and tanzanite.

Oil painting on lapis lazuli, *Perseus Rescuing Andromeda*, by Giuseppe Cesari.

Birth Flowers: December's flowers are the narcissus and the holly.

Illustration by Anton Hartinger from *Atlas der Alpenflora* (1882)

"December," by Eugène Grasset

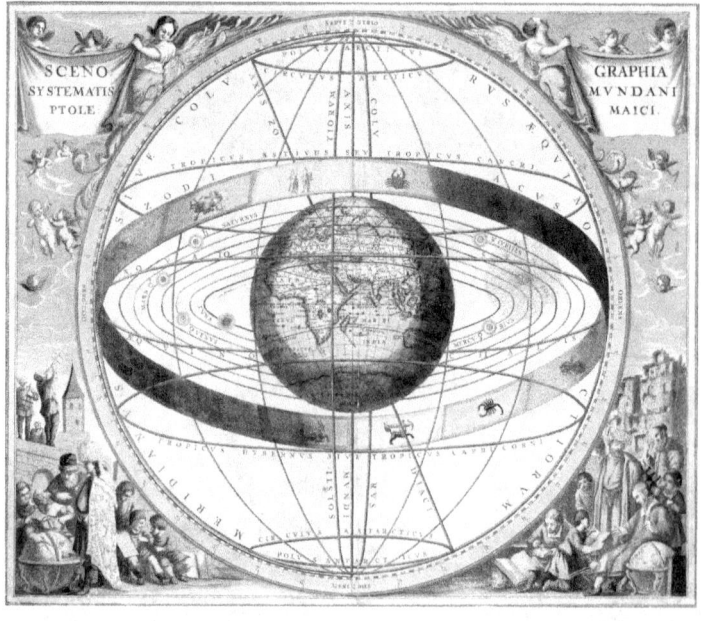

Scenography of the Ptolemaic Cosmography, by Johannes van Loon, based on Andreas Cellarius's *Harmonia Macrocosmica,* 1660

December 1 Zodiac Signs

From the perspective of someone on Earth, the Sun appears to move through the sky throughout the year, along a path astronomers call the *ecliptic plane*. The ecliptic plane is divided into twelve constellations, known as the zodiac, based on traditionally observed patterns of stars. On your birthday, you can't see your constellation, because it's in the daytime sky.

The zodiac was first developed by Babylonian astronomers about 2,500 years ago. Because they were unaware that the Earth wobbles like a spinning top (known as *precession*), they didn't make allowance for the fact that the Sun's path through the zodiac changes over time.

That means there are now two sets of dates for your birth sign. The *tropical dates* are the original Babylonian dates; the *sidereal dates* tell you where the Sun actually appears as it moves along its annual path.

For December 1, the tropical sign is **Sagittarius** and the sidereal sign is **Scorpio**.

Sagittarius

Tropical November 23 to December 21
Sidereal December 16 to January 14

Sagittarius means "archer" in Latin. The constellation in the night sky is often depicted as having the appearance of a stick-figure archer drawing its bow.

The brighter stars in Sagittarius form an asterism known as The Teapot. The Milky Way is densest in Sagittarius, because the galactic center lies in that direction.

In astrology, Sagittarius is a fire sign. People born under it are said to be not superstitious. They are supposed to be drawn toward travel and philosophy, and to enjoy social contacts, meeting new people, and exploring other cultures. They are also said to be highly intelligent, visionary, and tolerant.

Sagittarians are considered compatible with Aries, Leo, and Gemini, and to a lesser extent with Taurus and Virgo.

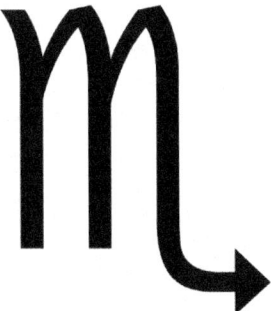

Scorpio

Tropical October 23 to November 21
Sidereal November 16 to December 15

Scorpio, the Scorpion, appears in the Greek myth of the hunter Orion. Because Orion had touched the robes of the goddess Artemis, in revenge, the goddess had the scorpion kill Orion. As a reward, she placed the scorpion in the sky, where it chases Orion through the eternal night.

The constellation of Scorpius includes the red giant star Antares, which is so large that the entire Solar System through the orbit of Mars would be inside it.

Scorpio is a fire sign, and people born under this sign are supposed to be determined, reserved, loyal, and secretive. Scorpios are supposed to be compatible with the water signs of Pisces and Capricorn.

Illustration by Edward Penfield

What Day of the Week is December 1?

On what day of the week does December 1 fall?

Surprisingly, this isn't an easy question. Because the calendar year is 365 days long (366 in leap years), it doesn't divide evenly by the seven days of the week.

Also, the Earth goes around the Sun in about 365-1/4 days, so a calendar tends to drift over time. That's why the same date falls on different weekdays in different years.

This is made even more complicated by a change in calendars that took place in 1582. Our modern calendar has its roots in ancient Rome, in a calendar reform conducted by Julius Caesar. Caesar commissioned mathematicians to attack the problem, and they came up with the idea of leap years, and thus standardized the calendar for centuries to come. This was called the Julian calendar.

Over time, however, the small errors in Caesar's calculation compounded. That's why Pope Gregory XIII commissioned the Gregorian calendar, used in most of the world today. Some countries converted in 1582, when the calendar was first developed; some converted later; other still haven't changed.

Gregorian and Julian aren't the only types of calendars. The Hebrew year, the Islamic year, and many other calendars are used in different parts of the world and among different people.

You can convert Gregorian dates to other calendars, including the Hebrew calendar, the Islamic calendar, and even the Mayan calendar by visiting the Fourmilab Calendar Converter at http://www.fourmilab.ch/documents/calendar/.

Chinese calendar systems are quite complex and have changed several times; a full discussion is far beyond the scope of this book. If you're interested, you can find information here: http://www.hermetic.ch/cal_stud/chinese_cal.htm.

On Names and Dates

Historians use "CE" (Common Era) and "BCE" (Before the Common Era) instead of the more common "AD" (Anno Domini, or Year of Our Lord) and "BC" (Before Christ), reflecting the fact that the year-numbering system established by the Gregorian calendar is used throughout the world in many countries not culturally Christian.

The CE/BCE designation dates back to at least 1708, and has been adopted as a standard by the United Nations and the Universal Postal Union. Because this series of books covers events and people of all nations and cultures, we use the CE/BCE terms.

The abbreviation "O.S." ("Old Style") and "N.S." ("New Style") on some dates refers to the fact that the Russian Empire (in particular) did not switch from the Julian to the Gregorian calendar at the same time as the rest of Europe, and therefore some figures and events have two dates.

Also, in the Julian calendar in England in the 16th century, the year began on March 25 rather than January 1. To avoid confusion with Gregorian dates, dates between January and March were often written using both years.

People and events whose original names are not in the Western alphabet have their native names (where possible) in the appropriate script shown in parenthesis. If you are using an e-reader to access an electronic version of this book, all characters don't always display on all devices.

A 50-year brass perpetual calendar.

Quote of the Day

"Time is an illusion, lunchtime doubly so."

Douglas Adams,
from *The Hitchhiker's Guide to the Galaxy*

Notes
and
Credits

THER
ACC
MAGNA

Timespinner
Press

Cartoon by John T. McCutcheon

Copyright, Credit, and Contact

Follow Us

Our blog "This Day in History" (http://
timespinnerpress.com/this-day-in-history/) features short
articles on events and people associated with each day, and
updates several times each week. Also subscribe to the
"Quote of the Day" at http://timespinnerpress.com/quote-
of-the-day/. You can get daily links by following us on
Facebook at TimespinnerPress, or on Twitter as
@sidewisethinker.

Contact Us

Find an error or a format problem? Want information about
the series, about us, or about when the volume for your
special day might be available? Please email us at
editor@timespinnerpress.com. (We also take requests if your
special day isn't yet complete. Please give us at least six
weeks' notice if possible.)

Sources

We owe a great debt to Wikipedia, which is our first stop for
research. We attempt to make independent confirmation of
all important dates and facts through a variety of other
sources.

Other sources we frequently use include the Library of
Congress; "on this day" listings from *Encyclopedia Britannica*,
the *New York Times*, and the BBC; Omniglot for the names of
months in other languages; *Chase's Calendar of Events*; and, of
course, the always essential Google.

All art and photographs are either in the public domain, used under a Creative Commons license, or with a "fair use" justification, and most frequently come from Wikimedia Commons and the Library of Congress Prints and Photographs Division.

Attribution is provided where possible, or as requested by the copyright owner, or when there is particular historical significance, listed below. For information about any particular illustration or photograph, please contact us.

Credits

1. The photograph of the bus ridden by Rosa Parks was taken by Alvin Trusty in 2015, and is used here under CC BY-SA 4.0. The bus itself can be found in the collection of the Henry Ford Museum, Dearborn, Michigan.

2. The illustration of the month of December used on the back cover is from the French Gothic illuminated manuscript *Les Très Riches Heures du duc de Berry* by the Limbourg Brothers, Jean Colombe, and an intermediate painter whose name is lost to history. It is in the public domain because its copyright has expired.

3. The box graphic used on the first page is from a 1916 pamphlet entitled "Divorce versus Democracy" authored by G. K. Chesterton, originally published in London by the Society of St. Peter and St. Paul. It is in the public domain in the US because it was published prior to 1923, and is in the public domain in all countries (including the country of origin) in which the copyright time is the author's life plus 70 years or less.

4. The graphic design for the section pages in this book is from a design originally created for a pharmacy label. It is courtesy of Wellcome Images (ICV No 11073, photo V0010813), and is used here under CC BY-SA 4.0.

5. The 1955 photograph of Rosa Parks with Dr. Martin Luther King, Jr., was originally published in *Ebony* magazine. It was taken on behalf of the United States Information Agency and is available from the US National Archives (ID 306-

PDS-65-1882, Box 93). It is in the public domain as a work created by an employee of the US government as part of that person's official duties.

6. The diagram of the Cleveland Avenue bus was entered as evidence in the court case of *Browder,et al. v. Gayle, et al.*, US District Court for the Middle District of Alabama, and is in the collection of the US National Archives (ARC 596069). It is in the public domain as a work prepared by an officer or employee of the US government as part of that person's official duties.

7. The 2012 photograph of President Barack Obama sitting in the Rosa Parks bus at the Henry Ford Museum was taken by White House photographer Pete Souza, and is in the public domain as a work created by an employee of the US government as part of that person's official duties. The image has been cropped.

8. The 1954 photograph of Christine Jorgensen was taken by Maurice Seymour. It is in the public domain because it was published in the United States between 1923 and 1977 without a copyright notice.

9. The photograph of Antarctica is an orthographic projection of NASA's Blue Marble data set, developed by Dave Pape in 2006, who released the image into the public domain.

10. The geographical profile of the Channel Tunnel was created in 2008 by Commander Keane, and is used here under CC BY-SA 4.0 and earlier licenses.

11. The 1955 portrait photograph of Alvin Ailey is by Carl Van Vechten as part of his "Creative Americans" series, and is in the public domain because of the deed of gift to the Library of Congress (digital ID van.5a51612).

12. The 1946 photograph of Michelini Bernardini modeling the first bikini is from the Hulton Archives, and its copyright status is unclear. Its use here falls under "Fair Use" provisions of the copyright code, because it represents a historical figure at a significant moment in fashion history, no free equivalent is available, and it is used at such a low resolution and reduced size as to make it unsuitable for the publication of counterfeit works.

13. The 1944 photograph of Georgy Zhukov on the cover of *Life* magazine was taken by Gregory Weil. It is in the public domain because it was published in the United States between 1923 and 1963 and although there was originally a copyright, the copyright was not renewed.

14. The publicity photo from the 1973 CBS special *Lily* is in the public domain because it was published in the United States between 1923 and 1977 and without a copyright notice. Traditionally, publicity photographs are not copyrighted because of the way in which they are intended to be used.

15. The publicity photo from the Broadway play *Play It Again, Sam* was taken sometime between 1969 and 1970. It is in the public domain because it was published in the United States between 1923 and 1977 and without a copyright notice. Traditionally, publicity photographs are not copyrighted because of the way in which they are intended to be used.

16. The 2010 photograph of Lee Trevino was taken by Keith Allison, and is used here under CC BY-SA 2.0.

17. The illustration of "The Red Bull" by Ronald McLeod first appeared in the December 1938 issue of *The American Magazine*, published by the Crowell Publishing Company. It is in the public domain because it was published in the United States between 1923 and 1963 and although there was an original copyright, the copyright was not renewed.

18. The 1952 photograph of David Ben-Gurion was cropped from a photograph by Pinn Hans. It can be found in the Israel National Photo Collection (item 69511, code D508-115). It is in the public domain in its country of origin because its term of copyright has expired according to the Israeli copyright statute of 2007.

19. The 1976 photograph of Stéphane Grappelli was taken by Allan Warren, and is used here under CC BY-SA 3.0.

20. The photograph of Aleister Crowley as a young man was created by "Magikritualnacht," and is used here under CC BY-SA 3.0.

21. The 1908 painting of the coronation of John IV of Portugal is by Veloso Salgado, and is in the collection of the Museu Militar (Sala Restauração), Lisbon. It is in the public domain because its copyright has expired.

22. The photograph of Prince Damrong Rajanubhab was taken sometime in the 1890s, and is in the public domain in its country of origin according to Sections 19–23 of the Thai Copyright Act, BE 2537 (1994), and is in the public domain in the United States because it was taken prior to January 1, 1923.

23. The painting "Landscape with Apple Tree" by Levi Wells Prentice was painted circa 1890, and is in the public domain because its copyright has expired.

24. The photograph of a bingo card was taken by Abbey Hendrickson, and is used here under CC BY-SA 2.0. It has been cropped.

25. The 2012 photograph of a large public advent calendar was taken by "Kora27" and is used here under CC BY-SA 4.0.

26. The artist who created the 19th century painting of a Hanukkah celebration is unknown. The image is in the public domain because its copyright has expired.

27. The painting "December" is from the *Brevarium Grimani*, circa 1510, and is in the public domain because its copyright has expired.

28. The etching "December" by Gabriel Perrelle was created circa 1660 and is in the public domain because its copyright has expired. The image is courtesy Wellcome Images, ICV No. 7850 BR, photo V0007629EBR, and is used here under CC BY-SA 4.0.

29. The 1815 woodcut of a proposal is in the public domain because its copyright has expired.

30. The 16th century oil on lapis lazuli painting *Perseus Rescuing Andromeda* is by Giuseppe Cesari. It is in the public domain because its copyright has expired. The original object is in the collection of the Saint Louis Art Museum.

31. The 1882 painting of *Ilex aquifolium* (holly) is by Anton Hartinger, and appeared originally in the book *Atlas der Alpenflora*.

32. The 1896 drawing "December" by Eugène Grasset is in the public domain because its copyright has expired.

33. The celestial sphere is from *Scenography of the Ptolemaic Cosmography*, by Johannes van Loon, based on Andreas

Cellarius's *Harmonia Macrocosmica*, 1660. It is in the public domain because its copyright has expired.

34. The 1906 automobile calendar is by Edward Penfield, and is in the collection of the Library of Congress Prints and Photographs Division. It is in the public domain because its copyright has expired.

35. The 50-year perpetual calendar photograph is in the public domain.

36. The cartoon by John T. McCutcheon is from his 1905 collection *The Mysterious Stranger and Other Cartoons by John T. McCutcheon*. It is in the public domain because its copyright has expired.

Timespinner
Press

License Description and Terms

Aside from material purely in the public domain, photographs and other material in this book are used under specific licenses permitting free use, usually with an attribution requirement. For full text and terms of these licenses, click or enter the appropriate links below. If you believe there is an error in the copyright status or attribution of any of these images, please email us.

- Creative Commons Attribution 2.0 Generic (CC-BY 2.0): http://creativecommons.org/licenses/by/2.0/deed.en
- Creative Commons Attribution-Share Alike 3.0 Generic (CC-BY-SA 3.0): http://creativecommons.org/licenses/by-sa/3.0/
- Creative Commons Attribution-Share Alike 2.5 Generic (CC-BY-SA 2.5): http://creativecommons.org/licenses/by-sa/2.5/deed.en
- Creative Commons Attribution-Share Alike 2.0 Generic (CC-BY-SA 2.0): http://creativecommons.org/licenses/by/2.0/deed.en
- Creative Commons Attribution-Share Alike 1.0 Generic (CC-BY-SA 1.0): http://creativecommons.org/licenses/by-sa/1.0/deed.en
- CC0 1.0 Universal (CC0 1.0) Public Domain Dedication (CC0 1.0) http://creativecommons.org/publicdomain/zero/1.0/deed.en
- GNU Free Documentation License (GFDL): http://en.wikipedia.org/wiki/Wikipedia:Text_of_the_GNU_Free_Documentation_License
- License Art Libre (Free Art License): http://artlibre.org

Other Books from Timespinner Press

The Story of a Special Day
Michael Dobson

A series of (eventually) 366 volumes covering everything that happened on your special day! Events, births, deaths, quotes, holidays, and much more. It's like a birthday card they'll never throw away!

US$7.95 print / US$2.99 ebook.

From Plassey to Pakistan
Humayun Mirza

The history of British Colonial India and the formation of Pakistan from the unique perspective of the son of Pakistan's first president and last of the royal line of Bengal, Bihar, and Orissa! This unique historical document tells the inside story of this distinguished family, including the detailed story of the coup that toppled his father from power!

US$27.95 print

A Whole New Navy: America's War in the Pacific

Miles Durr

The most comprehensive and detailed description of America's naval war in the Pacific ever—every battle, every ship, every task force and every task group from Pearl Harbor through the Japanese surrender! A must-have for the collection of every World War II buff!

US$29.95 print

Improbable History: The Weird, the Obscure, and the Strangely Important

edited by Michael Dobson

From the birth of Western civilization to the rescue of Apollo 13, from the Leaning Tower of Pisa to Florence's Duomo, history has often turned on small, improbable details. Whatever happened to the ancient Samaritan people? Why did a fortuitous rainstorm allow the British to conquer India? How did an air raid in Italy lead to the development of chemotherapy? What happened when Albert Einstein met Adolf Hitler on the streets of Berlin? How did the Japanese manage to attack the US mainland using balloons? A cast of award-winning writers tackle some of the strangest tales in history!

US$19.95 print